princess cupcakes

princess cupcakes

hamlyn

An Hachette UK Company
www.hachette.co.uk

First published in Great Britain in 2010 by
Hamlyn, a division of Octopus Publishing
Group Ltd
Endeavour House
189 Shaftesbury Avenue
London
WC2H 8JY
www.octopusbooks.co.uk

Distributed in the US by
Hachette Book Group USA
237 Park Avenue
New York, NY 10017
USA

Distributed in Canada by
Canadian Manda Group
165 Dufferin Street
Toronto, Ontario M6K 3H6
Canada

ISBN 978-0-600-62198-0

A CIP catalogue record for this book is available from the British
Library

Printed and bound in China

10 9 8 7 6 5 4 3 2

Both metric and imperial measurements are given for the recipes. Use
one set of measures only, not a mixture of both.

Standard level spoon measures are used in all recipes:
1 tablespoon = one 15 ml spoon
1 teaspoon = one 5 ml spoon

Ovens should be preheated to the specified temperature. If using a
fan-assisted oven, follow the manufacturer's instructions for adjusting
the time and temperature.

Eggs should be medium unless otherwise stated; choose free-range if
possible and preferably organic. The Department of Health advises
that eggs should not be consumed raw. This book contains some
dishes made with raw or lightly cooked eggs. It is prudent for more
vulnerable people, such as pregnant and nursing mothers, invalids,
the elderly, babies and young children, to avoid uncooked or lightly
cooked dishes made with eggs.

This book includes dishes made with nuts and nut derivatives. It is
advisable for those with known allergic reactions to nuts and nut
derivatives and those who may be potentially vulnerable to these
allergies, such as pregnant and nursing mothers, invalids, the elderly,
babies and children, to avoid dishes made with nuts and nut oils. It is
also prudent to check the labels of preprepared ingredients for the
possible inclusion of nut derivatives.

Contents

Introduction

If your daughter is a little princess (or if you just love all things pretty and pink yourself), then cupcakes are the perfect indulgence. Each little cake, with its soft, spongy base, creamy topping and sparkly decorations, is a tasty gem, fit for royalty. Kids love helping to make cupcakes — you can choose the flavour, customize the toppings and finish off your cakes with an array of sweets and gorgeous adornments.

This book is full of recipes for cupcakes that you and your little ones can bake together. From Chocolate Strawberry Cupcakes and Precious Pink Cupcakes for pampering and indulging, to Magic Wand Cupcakes and Marshmallow Cupcakes for special occasions and a Birthday Cake Stack for princess parties, there are countless recipes for pretty, delicious cakes.

First baking experiences
Children will learn an enormous amount from cooking without even realizing it. There's the coordination required to measure out ingredients, to mix, spoon out, beat and spread. Next, weighing and measuring introduce children to the concepts of numbers, weights, volume and accuracy. Lastly, there's the chemistry involved in the baking itself – the transforming effect of heat on food.

The recipes in this book are easy and quick, so you can bake in batches and share your baked goods with friends and family. If you are using silicone moulds, the cooking experience is even simpler – they are flexible, safe and can be used again and again.

The important thing when cooking with little children is to allow lots of time – children hate being hurried - and not to worry too much about the look of the results! It's the time spent creating something together that's important.

What can your child do?
Because cooking is an activity that uses all of the senses, it absorbs children totally. It gives them a sense of achievement and confidence, as they try new actions by themselves. Children will enjoy helping you in the kitchen from the time

they are old enough to stand on a chair and reach the worktop. Covering their hands with yours and letting them think they are cutting butter or spreading icing gives them a huge thrill and costs you nothing but patience.

Children develop at different rates, but between the ages of 3 and 6 you'll find that they can stir ingredients in a bowl and, under direction, add ingredients to the bowl. Over-6s will be able to use measuring spoons, measure liquids into a jug and beat ingredients with a whisk or wooden spoon.

Basic equipment

Cupcakes require only basic equipment. The following items are all you'll need to make a batch of delicious cakes, ready for decorating as simply or creatively as you like.

Using silicone moulds

Most of the recipes in this book can be made with 12 silicone moulds. Cake mixtures rise as they bake, so take care not to overfill the cases or the mixture will fall over the sides and make the sponge deflate. To avoid this, don't fill the cases more than about two-thirds full.

Some recipes make a mixture for more than 12 cakes. If baking more than 12 cakes, or if you have excess mixture and are not using a fan oven, bake in 2 separate batches rather than rotating the trays halfway through cooking as you might with cookies or meringues, because opening the oven halfway through cooking could make the cakes deflate.

Some recipes are better suited to different-sized cases or silicone moulds. You can use larger muffin cases if you prefer, or make in standard-sized cases or silicone moulds, being sure to reduce the cooking time slightly and keep an eye on the cakes throughout baking.

It's not always necessary to use baking sheets with silicone moulds, but they do support the paper cases particularly well. Below is some other equipment that may come in useful.

Silicone cases These are a safe and simple option for making cupcakes. Silicone is flexible, so it is easy for little hands to use and the cases can be bought in bright colours and novelty shapes. Reusable and dishwasher-proof as well as ovenproof, they can be positioned on a baking sheet for cooking rather than in tin sections. They do not absorb flavour or

taint food and they nest nicely together for easy storage. After use, wash and dry thoroughly before storing.

Cupcake tins These vary slightly, but are usually about the size that you'd use for baking individual jam tarts. The sections generally have sloping sides and are also available with a nonstick coating, which is useful if you're making little cakes without paper cases.

Muffin trays This type of tray has larger, deeper sections with straighter sides, ideal for making larger cupcakes for adult-sized portions. Muffin trays are also available with a nonstick coating.

Paper cake cases If you want to experiment with sizes, you can buy all kinds of paper cake cases, ranging from tiny fairy-cake cases to giant-sized muffin ones. Use whichever size you prefer, though of course if you are using a muffin case where a cake case is called for, you won't make as many cakes, and vice versa.

Cupcake stands Whether for a birthday party or another special occasion, piling up cupcakes on a tiered stand looks stunning and eliminates the need for cake cutting. These stands are available in easily assembled card or clear acetate, with pillars or separators to create the layers. Metal cupcake stands that incorporate individual sections to support each cupcake are a good choice for smaller gatherings. Look in cook shops or specialist cake-decorating shops, or on the internet, to find a variety of design options.

Step-up stool It's worth investing in a child's step-up stool or a child-sized chair so that your child can see above the worktop and/or have a low table that they can work on. Alternatively, they could sit on a clean floor or on a plastic sheet or tablecloth.

Apron An apron is a treat for small cooks. A wipe-clean one will make it particularly easy to avoid splashes and keep your child clean. A cheaper alternative is to use an old shirt (check out the charity shops) or even a plastic raincoat!

Digital weighing scales These are the easiest type of scales for children to use, as the numbers are clear and easy to read, and it's easier for children to match them exactly to what's given in the recipe book.

Small wooden spoon A child-sized wooden spoon makes beating and mixing much easier for very little ones.

Set of measuring spoons These are useful for accurately measuring ingredients in whole and fractions of teaspoons and tablespoons. Fill the spoons level – a rounded measure could almost double the amount of ingredient required! Don't use everyday spoons, as their designs, depths and shapes vary.

Plastic measuring jugs and bowls Plastic equipment is obviously better than glass for children's use, in case of clumsy hands.

Safety first

Small children must always be supervised in the kitchen. Teach them basic hygiene rules from an early age, as well as telling them about the potential dangers posed by hot ovens, full saucepans and sharp knives.

Hygiene Always wash hands before starting to cook and make sure surfaces are clean. Tie back long hair and wear an apron or coverall.

Ovens and hobs Take special care when opening oven doors in front of expectant young cooks and make sure they stand well back so they don't get blasted by hot air. Always use oven gloves. Also, be especially wary of recently turned-off but still very hot hobs. Use the back rings of the hob when working with small children so they are not tempted to grab saucepan handles from below to see what's cooking.

Sharp knives It's great to get young children involved in the clearing-up process and you can establish good working practices from the start. But make it a rule never to place any sharp knives or food processor blades in the sink, where they can easily be hidden by soap bubbles. Instead, wash them as you go and place knives straight back on a knife rack or in a drawer, and processor blades in their storage box, well out of harm's way.

Some simple techniques

Unlike larger cakes, which are more prone to sinking in the centre or being over- or undercooked, there's less that can go wrong when making cupcakes.

Mixing the basic sponge Some of the recipes in this book use the 'all-in-one' method, in which all the cake ingredients are beaten together in a bowl using a hand-held electric whisk or a wooden spoon. Make sure you've softened the butter beforehand (either gently in a microwave oven or by letting it stand at room temperature) so that the mixture creams together easily. This will take 3–4 minutes if you're using a wooden spoon. An alternative, more traditional, method is to cream the butter and sugar, beat in the eggs, then sift in the flour and gently fold it in, sometimes adding a little liquid so that the mixture forms a dropping consistency. Both methods can also be used in a free-standing electric mixer or a large food processor.

Making muffins Muffins are made by folding the 'wet' ingredients, such as eggs, melted butter and buttermilk or milk, into the dry ingredients, including the flour, baking powder, dried fruits and flavourings. Use a large metal spoon and fold the ingredients gently together until they're only just combined: overmixing the ingredients will produce a tougher texture. It does not matter if there are still traces of flour dispersed in the mixture.

Testing whether the cakes are cooked At the end of the cooking time, gently open the oven and lightly touch the top of 1 of the cakes. The cakes should have risen and the surface should feel soft but still firm to the touch. For a basic sponge mixture the crust should be pale golden. Avoid overcooking or the cakes will taste dry.

Cooling the cakes Most of the cupcakes are cooled before decorating. Leave them for a couple of minutes once you have taken them out of the oven, then carefully lift them on to a wire rack. Leave until completely cold before decorating, particularly if using whipped cream or buttercream. Some cakes, including muffin recipes and savoury cupcakes, are best served warm to enjoy their flavour at their best. Muffins don't keep well and any leftovers should be warmed through to refresh them before serving. Ideally, any that are not eaten freshly baked should be frozen for later use.

Storing cupcakes Cupcakes are best served freshly baked. However, if you are making them ahead, they'll keep well in an airtight container for 24 hours. If you are keeping them for more than a couple of days, it's best to freeze them, allowing them to thaw for several hours before decorating. Cakes decorated with buttercream or chocolate frosting can be frozen ready decorated, but those finished with whipped cream or icings are best decorated once thawed.

Piping decorations Ingredients such as whipped cream, meringue, melted chocolate and buttercream can be piped on to cupcakes for a more formal, uniform presentation rather than simply being spooned or spread with a knife.

Reusable nylon piping bags, available from specialist cake-decorating shops or cook shops, can be fitted with a star or plain piping nozzle for piping and then washed ready for reuse. For piping scribbled lines or more intricate decorations, a paper piping bag is an easier option. These can be bought ready made from good cake-decorating suppliers or you can make your own from triangles of greaseproof paper. The advantage of using a disposable piping bag is that you can have several different bags in use at one time, for example when using different-coloured icings for decoration. It also means that you can snip off the merest tip of the bag for piping without having to insert a plastic or metal nozzle. Take care not to snip off too much of the tip or the icing will flow out too thick and fast.

Making a paper piping bag Cut out a 25 cm (10 inch) square of greaseproof paper. Fold it diagonally in half. Cut the paper in half, just to one side of the folded line. Holding 1 piece with the long edge away from you, curl the right-hand point over to meet the centre point, making a cone shape. Bring the left-hand point over the cone so the 3 points meet. Fold the points over several times to secure the cone. Snip off the tip and insert a piping nozzle, if using. Half fill the bag with icing and fold over the end to secure.

Using writing icing Tubes of writing icing can be bought in many colours for use as a quick and easy cake decoration. Some come with changeable tips for piping.

Melting chocolate There are 3 ways of melting chocolate. When melted with butter or milk, the melting time will be reduced because of the high fat content of these additional ingredients.

To melt chocolate in a microwave oven: Chop the chocolate into small pieces and put in a microwave-proof bowl. Melt the chocolate in one-minute spurts, checking frequently. Take particular care when melting white or milk chocolate, as they have a higher sugar content and are more prone to scorching.

To melt chocolate in the oven: Chop the chocolate into small pieces and put in a small ovenproof dish or bowl. Put in the switched-off oven after baking and leave until melted.

To melt chocolate on the hob: Chop the chocolate into small pieces and put in a heatproof bowl. Set the bowl over a saucepan of gently simmering water, making sure the base of the bowl doesn't come in contact with the water. Once the chocolate starts to melt, turn off the heat and leave until completely melted, stirring once or twice until no lumps remain. It's crucial that no water (including steam) gets into the bowl or the chocolate will solidify and cannot be melted again.

Using ready-to-roll icing This soft, pliable icing is available from supermarkets, usually in white or basic colours, or in a wider range of colours from specialist cake-decorating shops or suppliers. It can be rolled out on a surface lightly dusted with icing sugar and cut into shapes using cutters or moulded like Plasticine into shapes. If opening a new slab of ready-to-roll icing, knead it lightly to soften it up before rolling out. White icing can be coloured by kneading in a few drops of liquid food colouring (to a pastel shade) or paste colouring (for a stronger shade). Any icing that's not in use should be wrapped tightly in clingfilm to prevent it drying out.

Using ready-made decorations These can range from supermarket-bought sugar sprinkles, tiny sweets and chocolates through to handmade edible flowers available from specialist cake-decorating shops or suppliers. You may want to check the ingredients used in some of the cheaper bought decorations before you buy them, or at least you may want to use them very sparingly.

Using writing icing Tubes of writing icing can be bought in many colours. Some come with changeable tips for piping.

Fillings and toppings

The following favourite fillings and toppings are used in the book and can also be used for other cupcake recipes of your choice. All 3 recipes are quick and easy to make, but the frostings take a little longer than the buttercream, as the chocolate needs to be melted.

Buttercream

Makes enough to cover 12 cupcakes
Preparation time 5 minutes

150 g (5 oz) unsalted butter, softened
250 g (8 oz) icing sugar, sifted
1 teaspoon vanilla extract
2 teaspoons hot water

Put the butter and icing sugar in a bowl and beat well with a wooden spoon or hand-held electric whisk until smooth and creamy. Add the vanilla extract and hot water and beat again until smooth.

Chocolate fudge frosting

Makes enough to cover 12 cupcakes
Preparation time 5 minutes
Cooking time 5 minutes

100 g (3½ oz) plain chocolate or milk chocolate, chopped
2 tablespoons milk
50 g (2 oz) unsalted butter
75 g (3 oz) icing sugar, sifted

1 Put the chocolate, milk and butter in a small, heavy-based saucepan and heat gently, stirring, until the chocolate and butter have melted.

2 Remove from the heat and stir in the icing sugar until smooth. Spread the frosting over the tops of cupcakes while still warm.

White chocolate fudge frosting

Melt the chocolate and milk (see pages 12–13). Remove the bowl from the pan and stir in the icing sugar until smooth. Spread the frosting over the tops of cakes while still warm.

Makes enough to cover 12 cupcakes
Preparation time 5 minutes
Cooking time 5 minutes

200 g (7 oz) white chocolate, chopped
5 tablespoons milk
175 g (6 oz) icing sugar, sifted

Vanilla cupcakes

Makes 12
Preparation time 10 minutes
Cooking time 20 minutes

150 g (5 oz) butter, softened
150 g (5 oz) caster sugar
175 g (6 oz) self-raising flour, sifted
3 eggs
1 teaspoon vanilla extract

1 Stand 12 silicone cupcake cases on a baking sheet or line a 12-section cupcake tin with paper or foil cake cases.

2 Put all the cake ingredients in a bowl and beat with a hand-held electric whisk or a wooden spoon until light and creamy. Divide the cake mixture between the cases.

3 Bake in a preheated oven, 180°C (350°F), Gas Mark 4, for 20 minutes or until risen and just firm to the touch. Transfer to a wire rack to cool.

Precious pink cupcakes

Makes 12

Preparation time 30 minutes,
plus cooling

Cooking time 20 minutes

125 g (4 oz) butter, softened

125 g (4 oz) caster sugar

2 eggs

50 g (2 oz) ground almonds

finely grated rind of 1 lemon

100 g (3½ oz) self-raising flour

½ teaspoon baking powder

For the buttercream

75 g (3 oz) unsalted butter, softened

150 g (5 oz) icing sugar, sifted

1 teaspoon vanilla extra

For the icing and decoration

125 g (4 oz) fondant icing
sugar, sifted

3–4 tablespoons lemon juice

a few drops of yellow food colouring

12 pink and white sugar flowers,
to decorate

1 Stand 12 silicone cupcake cases on a baking sheet or line a 12-section cupcake tin with paper or foil cake cases.

2 Put the butter, sugar, eggs, ground almonds and lemon rind in a bowl, sift in the flour and baking powder and beat with a hand-held electric whisk or a wooden spoon until light and creamy. Divide the cake mixture between the cases.

3 Bake in a preheated oven, 180°C (350°F), Gas Mark 4, for 20 minutes or until risen and just firm to the touch. Transfer to a wire rack to cool.

4 Put the unsalted butter, icing sugar and vanilla extract in a bowl and beat with a hand-held electric whisk or a wooden spoon until smooth. Place a teaspoonful of the buttercream on top of each cake and mould into a smooth dome using a knife.

5 Mix the fondant icing sugar in a separate bowl with enough lemon juice to make an icing that doesn't quite hold its shape. Stir in the food colouring. Place a teaspoonful on top of the buttercream. Ease the icing over the tops of the cupcakes to cover the buttercream completely. Decorate each cake with a pink and white sugar flower.

Magic wand cupcakes

Makes 12

Preparation time 40 minutes, plus
cooling and setting

Cooking time 25–30 minutes

100 g (3½ oz) butternut squash,
peeled and deseeded

125 g (4 oz) butter, softened

50 g (2 oz) light muscovado sugar

100 g (3½ oz) clear honey

2 eggs

50 g (2 oz) porridge oats

150 g (5 oz) self-raising flour

½ teaspoon baking powder

1 teaspoon ground mixed spice

For the icing and decoration

50 g (2 oz) orange ready-to-roll icing

50 g (2 oz) white ready-to-roll icing

200 g (7 oz) fondant icing sugar,
sifted, plus extra for dusting

2–3 tablespoons orange juice

4 tablespoons orange curd

indoor sparklers

1 Stand 12 silicone cupcake cases on a baking sheet or line a 12-section cupcake tin with paper or foil cake cases.

2 Grate the squash into a bowl, add the butter, light muscovado sugar, honey, eggs and porridge oats, then sift in the flour, baking powder and mixed spice. Beat with a hand-held electric whisk or a wooden spoon until light and creamy. Divide the cake mixture between the cases.

3 Bake in a preheated oven, 180°C (350°F), Gas Mark 4, for 25–30 minutes or until risen and just firm to the touch. Transfer to a wire rack to cool.

4 Roll out the orange and white icings on a worktop lightly dusted with fondant icing sugar and cut out 12 small star shapes, either by hand or using a cutter. Push a wooden cocktail stick into each and place on a sheet of greaseproof paper to harden for at least 1 hour.

5 Beat the fondant icing sugar in a bowl with 2 tablespoons of the orange juice, adding a little extra juice if necessary to give a thick but spreadable consistency. Spoon over the cakes, spreading to the edges. Take 1 teaspoon of the orange curd and pour it, in a loose spiral, over each cake. Push an icing star down into each cake. Just before serving, position the sparklers on the cakes and light.

Princess crown cupcakes

Makes 12

Preparation time 30 minutes,
plus cooling

Cooking time 20 minutes

1 quantity Buttercream (see page 14)

a few drops of pink food colouring

12 Vanilla Cupcakes (see page 16)

edible silver balls

1 Divide the buttercream mixture between 2 bowls. Add the food colouring to 1 bowl and mix well. Spread the pink buttercream over the tops of the cooled cakes to within 5 mm (¼ inch) of the edges using a small palette knife, doming it up slightly in the centre.

2 Put half the uncoloured buttercream in a piping bag fitted with a writing nozzle and the remainder in a piping bag fitted with a star nozzle. Pipe lines, 1 cm (½ inch) apart, across the pink buttercream, then across in the other direction to create a diamond pattern. Pipe little stars around the edges using the icing in the other bag. Decorate the piped lines with silver balls.

Daisy celebration cupcakes

Makes 24

Preparation time 1–1½ hours, plus cooling and setting

Cooking time 25 minutes

250 g (8 oz) butter, softened

250 g (8 oz) caster sugar

4 eggs

1 tablespoon vanilla extract

finely grated rind of 2 lemons

300 g (10 oz) self-raising flour

1 teaspoon baking powder

For the decoration

125 g (4 oz) pale pink ready-to-roll icing

icing sugar, sifted, for dusting

125 g (4 oz) deep pink ready-to-roll icing

300 ml (½ pint) double cream

300 g (10 oz) white chocolate, chopped into small pieces

1 Stand 24 silicone cupcake cases on 2 baking sheets or line 2 x 12-section cupcake tins with paper or foil cake cases.

2 Put the butter, caster sugar, eggs, vanilla extract and lemon rind in a bowl, sift in the flour and baking powder and beat until light and creamy. Divide the mixture between the cases.

3 Bake a batch in a preheated oven, 180°C (350°F), Gas Mark 4, for 20 minutes or until risen and just firm to the touch. Transfer to a wire rack to cool. Repeat for the second batch.

4 Roll out the pale pink icing on a worktop lightly dusted with icing sugar. Stamp out 12 flowers using a cutter about 4 cm (1¾ inches) in diameter. Cup each flower slightly in the palm of your hand and transfer to a sheet of crumpled foil to harden.

5 Roll out the deep pink icing and make 12 more flowers. Take a tiny piece of pale pink icing from the trimmings and press against a piece of tulle. Peel away the tulle. Press the icing gently into the centre of a deep pink flower. Repeat for the remaining flowers, alternating the pinks.

6 Put 200 ml (7 fl oz) of the cream in a saucepan and bring almost to the boil. Pour over the chocolate in a bowl and leave until it has melted, stirring occasionally until smooth. Leave to cool. Stir the remaining cream into the chocolate mixture and whip until just holding its shape. Pipe or spoon over the cakes. Decorate with the prepared flowers.

Very cherry cupcakes

Makes 12

Preparation time 20 minutes, plus cooling

Cooking time 25 minutes

100 g (3½ oz) whole blanched almonds

100 g (3½ oz) butter, softened

100 g (3½ oz) caster sugar

2 eggs

125 g (4 oz) self-raising flour

1 teaspoon baking powder

100 g (3½ oz) natural glacé cherries, quartered

4 tablespoons cherry jam or strawberry jam

For the icing and decoration

100 g (3½ oz) icing sugar, sifted

2–3 teaspoons water

6 cherries, halved and stoned, to decorate

1 Stand 12 silicone cupcake cases on a baking sheet or line a 12-section cupcake tin with paper or foil cake cases.

2 Put the almonds in a food processor and process until ground. Tip the ground almonds into a bowl and add the butter, caster sugar and eggs, then sift in the flour and baking powder. Beat well with a hand-held electric whisk or a wooden spoon until light and creamy, then stir in the glacé cherries. Divide the cake mixture between the cases.

3 Bake in a preheated oven, 180°C (350°F), Gas Mark 4, for 25 minutes or until risen and just firm to the touch. Transfer to a wire rack to cool.

4 Press the jam through a sieve to remove any lumps and spread over the tops of the cakes. Beat the icing sugar in a bowl with the water to make a thick icing that almost holds its shape. Spread a little over each cake and decorate with the cherry halves.

Rose delight cupcakes

Makes 12

Preparation time 15 minutes,
plus cooling

Cooking time 20 minutes

125 g (4 oz) butter, softened

125 g (4 oz) caster sugar

2 eggs

1 teaspoon vanilla extract

150 g (5 oz) self-raising flour

½ teaspoon baking powder

125 g (4 oz) rose-flavoured Turkish
delight, snipped into small pieces

For the topping

300 ml (½ pint) double cream

2 teaspoons rosewater

2 teaspoons icing sugar, sifted

seeds of 1 small pomegranate

1 Stand 12 silicone cupcake cases on a baking sheet or line a 12-section cupcake tin with paper or foil cake cases.

2 Put the butter, caster sugar, eggs and vanilla extract in a bowl, sift in the flour and baking powder and beat with a hand-held electric whisk or a wooden spoon until light and creamy. Stir in the Turkish delight, then divide the cake mixture between the cases.

3 Bake in a preheated oven, 180°C (350°F), Gas Mark 4, for 20 minutes or until risen and just firm to the touch. Transfer to a wire rack to cool.

4 Whip the cream in a bowl with the rosewater and icing sugar until just forming soft peaks. Swirl over the tops of the cakes with a small palette knife or pipe through a large star nozzle and scatter with the pomegranate seeds.

Banana treasure cupcakes

Makes 12

Preparation time 20 minutes plus cooling

Cooking time 25 minutes

125 g (4 oz) plain flour
1 teaspoon baking powder
¼ teaspoon bicarbonate of soda
75 g (3 oz) butter, melted
75 g (3 oz) light muscovado sugar
2 eggs, beaten
2 small, very ripe bananas, mashed

For the icing and decoration
100 g (3½ oz) unsalted butter, softened
5 tablespoons clear honey
5 tablespoons icing sugar, sifted
dried banana slices (optional)

1 Stand 12 silicone cupcake cases on a baking sheet or line a 12-section cupcake tin with paper or foil cake cases.

2 Sift the flour, baking powder and bicarbonate of soda into a bowl.

3 Put the melted butter, light muscovado sugar, eggs and mashed bananas in another bowl and beat together with a wooden spoon. Tip in the dry ingredients and mix together gently until evenly combined. Divide the cake mixture between the cases.

4 Bake in a preheated oven, 160°C (325°F), Gas Mark 3, for 25 minutes or until risen and just firm to the touch. Transfer to a wire rack to cool.

5 Put the unsalted butter, honey and icing sugar in a bowl and beat with a hand-held electric whisk or a wooden spoon until smooth and creamy. Spread the icing over the tops of the cakes using a small palette knife. Decorate with dried banana slices, if liked.

Butterfly cupcakes

Makes 12

Preparation time 25 minutes, plus cooling

Cooking time 20 minutes

12 Vanilla Cupcakes (see page 16)
1 quantity Buttercream (see page 14)

1 Cut out a circle from the centre top of each cooled cake neatly using a small, sharp knife. Cut each circle in half.

2 Put the buttercream in a big piping bag fitted with a large star nozzle. Pipe a large swirl of buttercream into the cavity of each cake. Reposition the 2 halves of the circles on each cake at an angle of 45° so that they resemble butterfly wings.

Chocolate strawberry cupcakes

Makes 12

Preparation time 30 minutes, plus cooling

Cooking time 30 minutes

75 g (3 oz) cocoa powder
225 ml (7½ fl oz) boiling water
125 g (4 oz) butter, softened
275 g (9 oz) light muscovado sugar
2 eggs
200 g (7 oz) plain flour
1 teaspoon baking powder

For the icing and decoration
150 ml (¼ pint) double cream
4 tablespoons icing sugar, sifted
4 tablespoons water
275 g (9 oz) plain chocolate, chopped
12 strawberries

1 Stand 12 silicone cupcake cases on a baking sheet or line a 12-section cupcake tin with paper or foil cake cases.

2 Put the cocoa powder in a heatproof bowl and whisk in the boiling water. Leave to cool.

3 Beat together the butter and muscovado sugar in a separate bowl with a hand-held electric whisk or a wooden spoon until pale and creamy. Add the eggs, beating after each addition, then sift in the flour and baking powder and gently fold them in with a large metal spoon before adding the cocoa mixture. Divide the cake mixture between the cases.

4 Bake in a preheated oven, 180°C (350°F), Gas Mark 4, for 25 minutes or until risen and just firm to the touch. Leave in the tin for 10 minutes, then transfer to a wire rack to cool.

5 Put the cream, icing sugar and water in a small saucepan and bring just to the boil. Remove from the heat and stir in 200 g (7 oz) of the chocolate. Leave to cool, stirring frequently until smooth and glossy.

6 Peel away the cases and spoon a little of the chocolate mixture over each cake, swirling it slightly down the sides using a small palette knife.

7 Melt the remaining chocolate (see pages 12–13), then half-dip the strawberries in the chocolate and position on the cakes.

Glitter pink cupcakes

Makes 12

Preparation time 20 minutes,
plus cooling

Cooking time 20 minutes

25 g (1 oz) sugared rose petals, plus
extra to decorate

125 g (4 oz) caster sugar

125 g (4 oz) butter, softened

2 eggs

1 tablespoon rosewater

150 g (5 oz) self-raising flour

½ teaspoon baking powder

For the frosting

250 g (8 oz) mascarpone cheese

125 g (4 oz) icing sugar, sifted

1 teaspoon lemon juice

a few drops of pink food colouring
(optional)

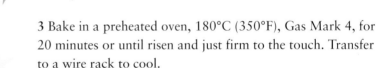

1 Stand 12 silicone cupcake cases on a baking sheet or line a 12-section cupcake tin with paper or foil cake cases.

2 Put the sugared rose petals and caster sugar in a food processor and process until the rose petals are chopped into small pieces. Tip into a bowl, add the butter, eggs and rosewater and sift in the flour and baking powder. Beat with a hand-held electric whisk or a wooden spoon until light and creamy. Divide the cake mixture between the cases.

3 Bake in a preheated oven, 180°C (350°F), Gas Mark 4, for 20 minutes or until risen and just firm to the touch. Transfer to a wire rack to cool.

4 Beat together the mascarpone, icing sugar, lemon juice and food colouring, if using, with a wooden spoon in a bowl until smooth. Spread the frosting over the tops of the cakes using a small palette knife and decorate with extra sugared rose petals.

Plum moon cupcakes

Makes 9

Preparation time 20 minutes

Cooking time 20–25 minutes

150 g (5 oz) polenta

100 g (3½ oz) caster sugar

1 teaspoon baking powder

75 g (3 oz) ground almonds

½ teaspoon almond extract

75 ml (3 fl oz) soured cream

3 tablespoons mild olive oil or vegetable oil

finely grated rind of 1 lemon

2 eggs

2 red plums, stoned and cut into thin wedges

4 teaspoons lemon juice

2 tablespoons clear honey

1 Stand 9 silicone cupcake cases on a baking sheet or line a 12-section cupcake tin with 9 paper or foil cake cases.

2 Put the polenta, sugar, baking powder and ground almonds in a bowl and mix together.

3 Put the almond extract, soured cream, oil, lemon rind and eggs in a separate bowl and mix until combined. Add to the dry ingredients and mix to a thick paste.

4 Divide the cake mixture between the cases and arrange a couple of plum wedges on top of each.

5 Bake in a preheated oven, 180°C (350°F), Gas Mark 4, for 20–25 minutes or until risen and beginning to colour around the edges. Leave to cool in the tin for a few minutes before transferring to a wire rack.

6 Pierce the tops of the cakes with a skewer. Mix together the lemon juice and honey and drizzle over the cupcakes while still warm.

Marshmallow cupcakes

Makes 12

Preparation time 25 minutes, plus cooling

Cooking time 25 minutes

125 g (4 oz) butter, softened

100 g (3½ oz) caster sugar

2 eggs

1 teaspoon vanilla extract

150 g (5 oz) self-raising flour

½ teaspoon baking powder

50 g (2 oz) marshmallows, snipped into pieces

For the topping

75 g (3 oz) marshmallows, snipped into pieces, plus extra to scatter

300 ml (½ pint) double cream

1 Stand 12 silicone cupcake cases on a baking sheet or line a 12-section cupcake tin with paper or foil cake cases.

2 Put the butter, sugar, eggs and vanilla extract in a bowl, sift in the flour and baking powder and beat with a hand-held electric whisk or a wooden spoon until light and creamy. Stir in the marshmallow pieces. Divide the cake mixture between the cases.

3 Bake in a preheated oven, 180°C (350°F), Gas Mark 4, for 20 minutes or until risen and just firm to the touch. Transfer to a wire rack to cool.

4 Put about one-third of the marshmallows for the topping in a small saucepan with half the cream. Heat very gently until melted. Tip into a bowl and leave to cool.

5 Whip the remaining cream in a bowl until just holding its shape. Stir in the marshmallow cream and remaining marshmallow pieces, then pile the topping on top of the cakes. Scatter with the extra chopped marshmallow pieces.

Raspberry surprise cupcakes

Makes 10

Preparation time 20 minutes

Cooking time 20 minutes

100 g (3½ oz) butter

75 g (3 oz) plain chocolate, at room temperature

100 g (3½ oz) ground almonds

125 g (4 oz) golden caster sugar

40 g (1½ oz) plain flour, sifted

3 egg whites

150 g (5 oz) raspberries

icing sugar, for dusting (optional)

1 Stand 10 silicone cupcake cases on a baking sheet or line a 12-section cupcake tin with 10 paper or foil cake cases.

2 Melt the butter in a small saucepan and leave to cool. Coarsely grate the chocolate – if the chocolate is brittle and difficult to grate, try softening it in a microwave oven for a few seconds first, but take care not to overheat and melt it.

3 Put the ground almonds, 75 g (3 oz) of the sugar and the flour in a large bowl and mix together. Stir in the melted butter and grated chocolate until just combined.

4 Whisk the egg whites in a thoroughly clean bowl until soft peaks form. Gradually whisk in the remaining sugar. Using a large metal spoon, fold half the egg whites into the chocolate mixture to lighten it, then fold in the remainder until evenly combined. Divide the cake mixture between the cases and scatter the raspberries on top.

5 Bake in a preheated oven, 200°C (400°F), Gas Mark 6, for 15 minutes or until golden and just firm to the touch. Transfer to a wire rack to cool. Serve dusted with icing sugar, if liked.

Pink alphabetti cupcakes

Makes 12

Preparation time 45 minutes,
plus cooling and setting

Cooking time 20 minutes

125 g (4 oz) butter, softened

125 g (4 oz) caster sugar

2 eggs

1 teaspoon vanilla extract

150 g (5 oz) self-raising flour

½ teaspoon baking powder

50 g (2 oz) white chocolate
polka dots

For the decoration

100 g (3½ oz) each of orange ready-
to-roll icing and red ready-to-roll
icing (or use other colours of
your choice)

icing sugar, sifted, for dusting

50 g (2 oz) white chocolate polka
dots, melted

1 Stand 12 silicone cupcake cases on a baking sheet or line a 12-section cupcake tin with paper or foil cake cases.

2 Put the butter, sugar, eggs and vanilla extract in a bowl, sift in the flour and baking powder and beat with a hand-held electric whisk or a wooden spoon until light and creamy. Stir in the polka dots. Divide the cake mixture between the cases.

3 Bake in a preheated oven, 180°C (350°F), Gas Mark 4, for 20 minutes or until risen and just firm to the touch. Transfer to a wire rack to cool.

4 Roll out the icing, one colour at a time, on a worktop lightly dusted with icing sugar and cut out small letter shapes using alphabet cutters. Transfer to a tray lined with baking parchment. Re-roll the trimmings to make more letters. Leave to set for at least 1 hour until dry and holding their shape.

5 Spread each cake with a thin layer of melted chocolate and scatter plenty of letters on top, if necessary securing them to one another with a dampened paintbrush.

Frosted flower cupcakes

Makes 12

Preparation time 40 minutes, plus cooling and setting

Cooking time 20 minutes

selection of small edible spring flowers, such as primroses, violets, rose petals or daisies

1 egg white

caster sugar, for dusting

1 quantity White Chocolate Fudge Frosting (see page 15)

12 Vanilla Cupcakes (see page 16)

fine pastel-coloured ribbon, to decorate (optional)

1 Make sure the flowers are clean and thoroughly dry before frosting. Put the egg white in a small bowl and beat lightly with a fork. Put the sugar in a separate bowl.

2 Use your fingers or a soft paintbrush to coat all the petals on both sides with the egg white. Dust plenty of sugar over the flowers until evenly coated. Transfer to a sheet of nonstick baking parchment and leave for at least 1 hour until firm to the touch.

3 Spread the chocolate frosting over the tops of the cooled cakes using a small palette knife. Decorate the top of each with the frosted flowers. Tie a length of ribbon around each paper cake case to decorate, finishing it with a ribbon bow, if using.

Lavender cupcakes

Makes 12

Preparation time 20 minutes,
plus cooling

Cooking time 20 minutes

6 lavender flowers, plus extra small
sprigs to decorate
125 g (4 oz) butter, softened
125 g (4 oz) caster sugar
finely grated rind of ½ orange
2 eggs
150 g (5 oz) self-raising flour
½ teaspoon baking powder

For the icing
150 g (5 oz) icing sugar, sifted
4–5 teaspoons orange juice
a few drops of lilac food colouring

1 Stand 12 silicone cupcake cases on a baking sheet or line a 12-section cupcake tin with paper or foil cake cases.

2 Pull the lavender flowers from their stems and put in a bowl with the butter, caster sugar, orange rind, eggs, flour and baking powder. Beat with a hand-held electric whisk for about a minute until light and creamy. Divide the cake mixture between the cases.

3 Bake in a preheated oven, 180°C (350°F), Gas Mark 4, for 20 minutes or until risen and just firm to the touch. Transfer to a wire rack to cool.

4 Mix the icing sugar with enough orange juice in a bowl to make a thin glacé icing. Colour with the food colouring. Spread over the cakes and decorate with small sprigs of lavender flowers.

Chocolate charm crunchies

Makes 20

Preparation time 15 minutes,
plus chilling

200 g (7 oz) dark chocolate, broken
into pieces
50 g (2 oz) butter
3 tablespoons golden syrup
125 g (4 oz) cornflakes
mini marshmallows, sliced,
to decorate

1 Stand 20 cake cases on a baking sheet.

2 Put the chocolate in a saucepan with the butter and golden syrup. Heat gently, stirring occasionally, until the chocolate and butter have completely melted and the mixture is smooth and glossy.

3 Stir in the cornflakes and mix until completely coated in the chocolate. Spoon the cornflake mixture into the cases and chill for 2–3 hours until firm to the touch. Decorate with sliced mini marshmallows.

Angel dust cupcakes

Makes 12

Preparation time 20 minutes,
plus cooling

Cooking time 45–60 minutes

sunflower oil, for brushing

275 g (9 oz) young rhubarb, trimmed
and cut into 1 cm (½ inch) lengths

175 g (6 oz) light muscovado sugar

150 g (5 oz) butter, softened

3 eggs

175 g (6 oz) self-raising flour

1 teaspoon baking powder

½ teaspoon ground cinnamon

For the topping

25 g (1 oz) butter, softened

50 g (2 oz) self-raising flour

25 g (1 oz) light muscovado sugar

3 tablespoons flaked almonds

icing sugar, for dusting

1 Stand 12 silicone cupcake cases on a baking sheet or line a 12-section cupcake tin with paper or foil cake cases.

2 Brush a foil-lined baking sheet lightly with oil and scatter with the rhubarb. Sprinkle with 25 g (1 oz) of the light muscovado sugar.

3 Bake in a preheated oven, 200°C (400°F), Gas Mark 6, for 20–30 minutes or until tender and beginning to darken around the edges. Leave to cool. Reduce the oven to 180°C (350°F), Gas Mark 4.

4 Put the remaining sugar, the butter and eggs in a bowl, sift in the flour, baking powder and cinnamon and beat with a hand-held electric whisk or wooden spoon until light and creamy. Divide the cake mixture between the cases, spreading it fairly level, and top with the rhubarb pieces.

5 Put the butter and flour for the topping in a food processor and whiz until the mixture resembles coarse breadcrumbs. Add the sugar and process briefly until mixed. Scatter over the cakes and sprinkle with the almonds.

6 Bake for 25–30 minutes until risen and golden. Transfer to a wire rack to cool. Serve dusted with icing sugar.

Rich velvet cupcakes

Makes 12

Preparation time 20 minutes,
plus cooling

Cooking time 20–25 minutes

50 g (2 oz) butter, softened

100 g (3½ oz) caster sugar

1 egg

50 g (2 oz) raw beetroot, peeled and
finely grated

150 g (5 oz) self-raising flour

2 tablespoons cocoa powder

½ teaspoon bicarbonate of soda

100 ml (3½ fl oz) buttermilk

1 teaspoon vinegar

For the frosting and decoration

200 g (7 oz) full-fat cream cheese

2 teaspoons vanilla extract

300 g (10 oz) icing sugar, sifted

12 cherries, to decorate

1 Stand 12 silicone cupcake cases on a baking sheet or line a 12-section cupcake tin with paper or foil cake cases.

2 Put the butter and sugar in a bowl and beat with a hand-held electric whisk or a wooden spoon until light and creamy, then beat in the egg and beetroot.

3 Sift the flour, cocoa powder and bicarbonate of soda together into a bowl. Tip half of the mixture into the creamed mixture and stir in gently with a wooden spoon.

4 Mix together the buttermilk and vinegar in a jug. Add half the liquid to the bowl and stir well. Stir in the remaining flour mixture, then the remaining liquid. Divide the cake mixture between the cases.

5 Bake in a preheated oven, 180°C (350°F), Gas Mark 4, for 20–25 minutes or until risen and just firm to the touch. Transfer to a wire rack to cool.

6 Put the cream cheese in a bowl and beat with a wooden spoon until softened. Beat in the vanilla extract and icing sugar until smooth. Swirl over the tops of the cakes and decorate each with a cherry.

Jewelled chocolate cupcakes

Makes 12

Preparation time 20 minutes, plus cooling

Cooking time 15 minutes

125 g (4 oz) butter

125 g (4 oz) light muscovado sugar

2 eggs

100 g (3½ oz) wholemeal self-raising flour

1 tablespoon cocoa powder

2 tablespoons milk

For the icing and decoration

100 g (3½ oz) redcurrants

300 g (10 oz) golden icing sugar, sifted

12 sprigs of 2–3 redcurrants, to decorate

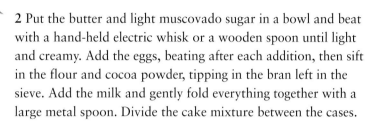

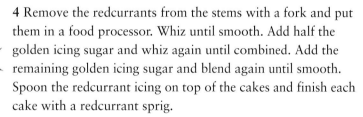

1 Stand 12 silicone cupcake cases on a baking sheet or line a 12-section cupcake tin with paper or foil cake cases.

2 Put the butter and light muscovado sugar in a bowl and beat with a hand-held electric whisk or a wooden spoon until light and creamy. Add the eggs, beating after each addition, then sift in the flour and cocoa powder, tipping in the bran left in the sieve. Add the milk and gently fold everything together with a large metal spoon. Divide the cake mixture between the cases.

3 Bake in a preheated oven, 200°C (400°F), Gas Mark 6, for 15 minutes or until risen and pale golden. Transfer to a wire rack to cool.

4 Remove the redcurrants from the stems with a fork and put them in a food processor. Whiz until smooth. Add half the golden icing sugar and whiz again until combined. Add the remaining golden icing sugar and blend again until smooth. Spoon the redcurrant icing on top of the cakes and finish each cake with a redcurrant sprig.

Glamour heart cupcakes

Makes 12

Preparation time 30 minutes, plus cooling

Cooking time 20 minutes

200 g (7 oz) icing sugar, sifted, plus extra for dusting

4–5 teaspoons rosewater or lemon juice

12 Vanilla Cupcakes (see page 16)

100 g (3½ oz) red ready-to-roll icing

6 tablespoons strawberry jam

1 Put the icing sugar in a bowl and add 4 teaspoons of the rosewater or lemon juice. Mix until smooth, adding a little more liquid if necessary, until the icing forms a thick paste. Spread over the tops of the cooled cakes.

2 Knead the red icing on a worktop lightly dusted with icing sugar. Roll out thickly and cut out 12 small heart shapes using a cutter. Place a heart on the top of each cake.

3 Press the jam through a small sieve to remove any lumps. Put the sieved jam in a small piping bag fitted with a writing nozzle. Pipe small dots into the icing around the edges of each cake and pipe a line of jam around the edge of each heart.

Christmas princess cupcakes

Makes 12

Preparation time 20 minutes,
plus cooling

Cooking time 20–25 minutes

125 g (4 oz) butter, softened
25 g (1 oz) dark muscovado sugar
2 eggs
1 tablespoon milk
150 g (5 oz) self-raising flour
½ teaspoon baking powder
1 teaspoon ground mixed spice
300 g (10 oz) luxury mincemeat

For the topping and decoration
300 ml (½ pint) double cream
2 tablespoons icing sugar, sifted
edible pink and silver balls,
to decorate

1 Stand 12 silicone cupcake cases on a baking sheet or line a 12-section cupcake tin with silver or gold foil cake cases.

2 Put the butter, dark muscovado sugar, eggs and milk in a bowl. Sift in the flour, baking powder and mixed spice and beat with a hand-held electric whisk or a wooden spoon until light and creamy. Add the mincemeat and stir in until evenly mixed. Divide the cake mixture between the cases

3 Bake in a preheated oven, 180°C (350°F), Gas Mark 4, for 20-25 minutes or until risen and just firm to the touch. Transfer to a wire rack to cool.

4 Put the cream and icing sugar in a bowl and whip until the mixture only just holds its shape. Pile the cream over the cakes and scatter with pink and silver balls to decorate.

Birthday cake stack

Makes 18

Preparation time 25 minutes,
plus cooling

Cooking time 20 minutes

175 g (6 oz) butter, softened

175 g (6 oz) golden caster sugar

3 eggs

finely grated rind of 2 lemons

200 g (7 oz) self-raising flour

1 teaspoon baking powder

For the buttercream and decoration

125 g (4 oz) unsalted butter, softened

200 g (7 oz) icing sugar, sifted

a few drops of pink food colouring
or blue food colouring

125 g (4 oz) small sweets, such as
dolly mixture and jellies

sugar sprinkles (optional)

birthday candles and candleholders
(optional)

1 Stand 18 silicone cupcake cases on 2 baking sheets or line 2 x 12-section cupcake tins with 18 paper or foil cake cases.

2 Put the butter, golden caster sugar, eggs and grated lemon rind in a bowl. Sift in the flour and baking powder and beat with a hand-held electric whisk or a wooden spoon until light and creamy. Divide the cake mixture between the cases.

3 Bake the first batch in a preheated oven, 180°C (350°F), Gas Mark 4, for 20 minutes or until risen and just firm to the touch. Transfer to a wire rack to cool. Repeat for the second batch.

4 Put the unsalted butter and icing sugar in a bowl and beat with a hand-held electric whisk or a wooden spoon until smooth and creamy. Beat in the food colouring. Spread the buttercream over the cooled cakes using a small palette knife. Decorate the cakes with plenty of small sweets and sugar sprinkles, if liked.

5 Arrange a layer of cakes on a serving plate and stack another 2 or 3 tiers on top. Push the required amount of birthday candles and candleholders into the cakes, if using.

Index

Acknowledgements

Executive Editor Eleanor Maxfield
Managing Editor Clare Churly
Creative Director Tracy Killick
Designer Miranda Harvey
Picture Library Manager Jennifer Veall
Production Controller Linda Parry

Photography: **Octopus Publishing Group**/Stephen Conroy 12; /David Munns 2, 7, 8 top, 8 bottom, 10, 11, 13, 15, 17, 19, 20, 25, 26, 29, 31, 35, 37, 39, 40, 43, 44, 47, 49, 53, 55, 56, 61, 63; /Gareth Sambidge 1, 23, 32, 58; /William Shaw 50. Cover: **Octopus Publishing Group**/David Munns.